CHIANTI

Nature, Environment and History

Text by
Giuliano VALDES

Photographs by
Giuliano VALDES

Published by
ITALCARDS
bologna Italy

Sole distributor for Siena and its province
C.N.C.
Località Valcanoro ☎ 055/80.78.424
Barberino Val d'Elsa (FI)

Introduction

If Tuscany, taken as a whole, is known and loved for the richness of its artistic, cultural, historical and landscape merits, probably not everybody is familiar with its great rich rural heart: but the name Chianti doesn't just give concrete form to the image of its noble and sublime product par excellence: the wine that has made this corner of Tuscany famous throughout the world. This ancient land represents the soul of Tuscany, which seems (even with the modernization introduced by the consumer society) to have stood still in time to the point where it has gained an almost 'fantastic' dimension, half-way between reality and legend. Beautiful and fascinating, the Chianti region is situated a little further beyond the first hilly spurs which mark the southern boundaries of the Florentine basin; the same thing can be said for the northern limits which are to be found immediately outside the walls of Siena.

The natural barycentre of Tuscany, Chianti has always been a desired and fought-over territory for the two powerful cities, which today, share one of the richest and most important tourist areas of Italy. The delicate equilibrium of long ago, due to the battles between the Florentines and the Sienese, fought out for a long time between their armies, and for almost the whole of the Medieval period, the history of these fertile regions was marked by bloody armed battles and long unending wars. The historical vicissitutes of the Chianti region have therefore put an unforgetable stamp on the places and on the countryside which, still today, bear the tangible signs of the past, as seen by the names of the localities, the villages and by the building features of a marked castle-type nature. A visit to the Chianti region calls for more attention than one would first imagine; if the nearby towns of Florence and Siena together with San Gimignano and many other towns of Tuscany have a strong tourist attraction, one shouldn't forget the small villages and towns of the Chianti region and also the parishes, the castles and the fortified hamlets which make up an endless source of artistic and architectural treasures to be discovered, and which are concealed in great numbers throught the entire region. Amongst the numerous proposals that the so-called 'Minor Tuscany can offer the visitor, the Chianti region excels in its range of natural environments, farms, in the very roots of Tuscany which here acquire particular qualities which, elsewhere, seem dull, if not completely cut off from the frantic pace of the mundane daily round.

It is not just by chance that this unique corner of Tuscany has been chosen as a permanent or seasonal residence by a great number of foreigners, attracted by the irresistible fascination of the undulating sequences of knolls and hills along which, stretch out as far as the eye can see, the most appreciated and famous vines in the world. If the vine plays an important role in the landscape and in the economy of the place, mention should be made immediately of the olive and the cypress, which are the other important elements of a vegetation which includes amongst its species, the chestnut, the maritime pine the oak and the cedar of Lebanon. In the places where the characteristics of the enviroment present harsher aspects of morphology, due to the stony soil, it isn't unusual to find vast areas of land used for grazing, alternated with woods which cover the highest slopes of the reliefs.

In this magical and fascinating microcosm one can trace the history of Man himself, who, as far back as the dawning of civilization, chose this as a land in which to settle down, and transformed it in order to meet his own economic needs. There are very few other areas in Italy where the aspects of a humanized countryside faithfully reflect the millenary activity of man, his hard work, his conquests, his ferocious battles for the possession and the subjection of lands and castles. The parishes and the churches are inserted like gems in an architectonic and urbane web of notable worth. Behind the Romanesque façades are hidden, not only an authentic popular religiousness, but also the tangible expression of notable works from an architectonic point of view and considerable art treasures too often ignored because of the label 'minor' which has been given to them.

The purpose of this guide is to indicate some of the most notable aspects of the rightly-named Chianti area, taking in some areas of its outermost districts, nowadays universally referred to by this name (i.e. Chianti). After a brief introduction on the geography and the climate of the area, we have dedicated some space to the individual communes, described in alphabetical order and also to the most important spots of interest to the tourist.

Finally we come to the history of the region: we will refer to this in the descriptions of the individual localities. We should like to briefly mention here that root of the actual place name probably derives from the Etruscan 'Clante' and the Etruscans were certainly the first people to inhabit the area, as proved by the noteworthy abundance of archeological findings. However the documents which refer to the area in Roman times are scarce and fragmentary. The first official mention of Chianti is contained in acts which date back to the 13th century and refers to a precise geographical area. All the historical events of the place between the 12th and the 15th century are permeated by the long battles between Florence and Siena for the supremacy of the territory. At the beginning of the 8th century Florence created the 'Lega del Chianti' (The League of Chianti), which under the emblem of the Gallo Nero (Black Cockrel) (which afterwards became famous) would then reunite the communes of Castellina, Gaiole and Radda. In the middle of the 16th century the Fall of the Sienese Republic sanctioned the Florentine rule.

The story of the Chianti wine also has very remote origins if we consider that the Canaiolo nero (one of the four grapes that make up Chianti wine) was defined as 'vitis vinifera Etruriae'. In the last century the baron Bettino Ricasoli worked out the proportions to be used in the mixing of the grapes coming from the vines of the Sangiovese, Canaiolo nero, Trebbiano toscano and Malvasia del Chianti. More recently the noble wine is connected to the history of the 'Consorzio of the Gallo Nero', which since 1924 is used for the identification and the protection of its product which today boasts the DOCG label (denomination controlled and guaranteed at origin). The boundaries of the so-called 'Chianti Classico' incorporate the communes of Greve in Chianti, Castellina in Chianti, Radda in Chianti, Gaiole in Chianti and parts of the communes of San Casciano Val di Pesa, Tavarnelle Val di Pesa, Barberino Val d'Elsa, Poggibonsi and Castelnuovo Berardenga. This wine producing area has been recognized as the oldest of its kind, even according to written testimony dating back to the 14th century and by a proclamation of the Grand duchy of Tuscany (18th century).

A view of the rural countryside of the Chianti region.

Chianti - Geographical and climatic aspects

The natural-historical subregion of Tuscany, it is situated between the provinces of Florence and Siena and occupies a wide stretch of territory which is prevalently hilly and mountainous, inserted between the drainage-basins of the Arno and the Ombrone. Its boundaries are not clearly marked, with exception to the eastern side, whose boundaries are marked by the so-called Mountains of Chianti where we find the highest point: Mount San Michele, 893 m. In other regions the territorial boundaries of Chianti extend as far as the rivervalleys of Arbia, Else, Greve and Pesa. From an administrative point of view, the Chianti region incorporates the whole Commune of the Chianti Classico (Greve in Chianti, Castellina in Chianti, Gaiole in Chianti) and also parts of the communal territories of San Casciano Val di Pesa, Barberino Val d'Elsa, Tavarnelle Val di Pesa, and Castelnuovo Berardenga. In the aptly-named Chianti region a small portion of the communal territory of Poggibonsi is also included. It's interesting to observe that alongside the 'Chianti Storico' (that which includes the historical communes of the Florentine 'League of Chianti') exists the 'Chianti Geografico', whose boundaries are marked by a triangle of land whose sides are made up of Valdarno between Florence and Arezzo, the Arezzo-Siena road and the Florence-Siena dual-carriageway.

The geological formation of the Chianti regions date back to the Eocene and Cretaceous periods. The brown and red schistic formations appartain to the former period, whilst to the latter period belong the areanaceous (sandy) formations (serein stone, sandstone, and hard sandstone), the formations of clay schists and the formations of marly-calcareous. A great amount of limestone is to be found here, belonging to the marly-calcareous formations and widely used in the construction of buildings, as well as the clay-schist formations, known locally as 'marls'.

From an economic point of view one sees a substantial homogenity throughout the whole territory, which is a natural and ideal area for wine-growing, along with the other special crop of Tuscany: the olive. In the last ten years, the Chianti region has witnessed an incredible growth in the sectors connected with the 'agrituristico' (holidays in farm-houses etc.) phenomenon whilst the more traditional kind of tourism has found an extremely favourable spot in this area, above all on the part of foreign tourists. As far as the services, and the service sector in general are concerned, due to the absence of a locality which carries out all the functions of a chief town, the Chianti area gravitates around the outlying centres of Florence, Siena and Poggibonsi.

When we talk about climate we should above all remember that the characteristics of the microclimate of the Chianti area, which is so favourable for wine and olive oil, are a reflection of the Tuscan climate in general. Because of the pleasant geographical position, which shelters the region from the cold Northern currents (normally protected by the natural barrier of the Apennines) and also thanks to the fact that the region is in an area which is not too far from the sea, the climate is generally quite mild throughout all the seasons of the year. The greatest amount of rainfall occurs in late autumn and in the first months of the year; the presence of both frost and snow is rare and quite exceptional. The average annual figures for the temperature are around 14 - 15° C. In summer the heat rarely exceeds 35° and the days are often mild due to the summer storms, which are quite frequent in the internal areas of Tuscany. In the winter months the north-east winds prevail, above all the 'Tramontana', which, although cold and biting, contributes in exhalting the landscape virtues of the Chianti environment, making the air particularly limpid and clear.

1. A view of the countryside in summer; 2. Typical countryside in the Chianti region; 3. San Casciano Val di Pesa, the Convent of St. Francis.

1. Greve in Chianti, Parish Church of S. Leolino; 2. The countryside near Tignano; 3. San Donato in Poggio the Castle; 4. Radda in Chianti a house with adjoining tower.

4

5

6

1. The countryside in winter; 2. A view of the Castle of Spaltenna; 3. S. Gusmè, the church of S.S. Cosma and Damiano; 4. Rural dwellings at S. Sano; 5. A typical shrine in the Chainti area; 6. The countryside around the commune of Barberino.

1

2

3

4

5

On the previous pages: a view of the typical Tuscan countryside; 1. Castle of Mugnana, portal with coats of arms; 2. A view of the surrounding countryside in summer; 3. The countryside near S. Leonino; 4. Basilica of S. Lucchese, the cloister; 5. A farm near S. Gusmè; 6. Molino di Botti, a typical example of the rural buildings in Chianti; 7. A view of the summer crops.

10

6

7

11

BARBERINO VAL D'ELSA

The commune of Barberino Val d'Elsa has 3.340 inhabitants and is set on a hilly plateau, and stretches along the hills between the river courses of Elsa and Pesa. The chief town is situated outside the confines of the Chianti Classico, even if parts of the communal territory are in fact contained within it. The locality faithfully imitates the lay-out of the typical Medieval fortified villages and contains aspects of notable architectonic, urban and enviromental interest.

The first mention of the village can be found in acts which date back to the middle of the 11th century, even if the first reference to Barberino goes back to before the destruction of Semifonte, carried out by the Florentines in the 13th century. The construction of the first urban settlement dates back to that time, which was then fortified by walls to protect it from the powerful neighbouring city. The Florentine Republic made it into a Medieval podestà which also became the chief town of the League of Barberino. In 1312 it was beseiged by the imperial armies of Arrigo VII; after once again acquiring its freedom, it ended up sharing the historical Florentine vicissitudes.

One notes the **town walls** which date back to the 14th century, in which are included two town gates, the most famous being *Porta Senese*, surmounted by a delightful belltower. Nearby stands the **Palace of Da Barberino**, a probatory and refined testimony of 14th century Medieval architecture. The **Magisterial Palace** is rendered typical by its façade which is decorated with the coats of arms of the podestà.

Nearby stands the **Parish church of S. Bartolomeo**, inside which one can admire pieces of a 14th - 15th century fresco depicting the *Annunciation*. The rectory contains a bronze bust of Pietro Tacca (*beato Davanzato*). In the 14th century **Hospital of the Pilgrims** are conserved frescoes of great value.

The **Town Hall** contains a painting which probably comes from the workshop of Bicci di Lorenzo, depicting the *Madonna with Child and Saints*, as well as archeological findings and material which date back to the Etruscan period.

1. Castle of Paneretta; 2. A view of Linari; 3. A view of the countryside around Tignano; 4. A view of Barberino Val d'Elsa.

3

4

On the opposite page: Barberino Val d'Elsa, the enchanting Sienes Gate with its striking medieval characteristics. 1. Tignano, views of the medieval village; 2. Barberino Val d'Elsa, a view of Via Barberini; 3. Barberino Val d'Elsa, the Parish Church.

1

2

Recommended excursions in the vicinity

Castle of Petrognano, the castle which today is private property still bears some details of the original ancient construction. The mighty ashlar tower built of square hewn stones is particularly outstanding; inside the castle we can see interesting and characteristic furnishings. In ancient times it was the possession of the Capponi family.

Castle of Tignano, the ruins of this powerful fortified building stand at the gate of the village bearing the same name, and this represents one of the most characteristic models of the vast typology of Medieval centres in the Chianti regions. Its construction dates back to the 11th century and for a long time the building made up part, together with the nearby fortress of Barberino, of the complex of Florentine defense structures of the castle which was subjected to a siege and captured by Arrigo VII remain only the ruins of the walls and a collapsed tower.

The Parish Church of S. Appiano, the building is certainly the most important monument in the district of Barberino. In front of the façade some columns act as proof of the existence of an ancient *Baptistery* (5th century), dismantled due to a schism at the beginning of the last century. Already mentioned in the 8th century, the parish church can be dated back to a period between the 12th and the 13th centuries, even if there are some structural elements present which date back to the 10th century. The interior, divided into three parts, contains frescos dating back to the 15th century dipicting the *SS. Domenico, Sebastiano, Antonio the Abbot and Matthew and the Madonna at prayer*. One can also see some precious 14th - 16th century silver and the *Gherardini tomb* (14th century). Near the parish church is an enchanting small cloister onto which looks out an extremely interesting Medieval-style hall, which was once part of the ancient feudal complex.

Castle of Linari, the castle, as it stands today, is the product of an almost completely new lay out. Architectonically it is extremely important, and is characterized by the elegant embattled tower with its ceiling and jutting brackets, but as a whole it stands out because of its outstanding values as a building. Already mentioned as far back as the 11th century, it was subjected to various vicissitudes and although it nearly always remained a Florentine possession it was conquered by the Visconti family in the 15th century and was afterwards subjected to the domination of Niccolò da Tolentino.

La Paneretta, this rambling farm, the property of one of the most noted Florentine families, became part of an ancient manor which had already been restructured towards the end of the 16th century. The building is a fortified construction whose walls are surmounted by Guelph merlons and which are strenghened by some corner towers. In the inner courtyard dominated by the imposing central keep one can see frescoes carried out during the 16th century by Bernardino Barbatelli known as '*il Poccetti*'. The castle has elements of extremely interesting architectonic character even within its interiors.

1. A view of the countryside around Barberino in winter; 2. Typical crops growing in the Chianti region near Linari; 3. Tignano; the remains of the medieval castle; 4. Castle of Petrognano, with the dome of S. Michele in the background; 5. Tignano, a view of the medieval village.

On the opposite page: Parish Church of S. Appiano, the small inner cloister; 1. Barberino Val d'Elsa, a view of the medieval walls; 2. Castle of Paneretta; 3. A view of the Castle of Linari.

19

3

1. Castle of Paneretta, a view of the building; 2. An old fashioned hearse near the Parish Church of S. Appiano;. 3. In the peaceful Chianti countryside stand the remains of an ancient Baptistry which faces the Parish Church of S. Appiano.

21

CASTELLINA IN CHIANTI

The commune of Castellina in Chianti has 2.545 inhabitants; the chief town is laid out on the summit of an ondulating and verdant hilly spur which separates the drainage basins of Pesa and Staggia, giving wide scenic views of the delightful surrounding countryside.

The history of Castellina dates back to the Etruscan period and this can be demonstrated by the discovery of a vast tumulus situated on a hill which dominates the modern town. In Medieval times the locality was controlled by the Guidi Counts (12th century) and was then afterwards enclosed by fortifications built by the Florentines, who made it into one of the strongholds of the 'League of Chianti', with the clear intention of holding the vindications of the Sienese at bay. The latter, however, took possession of the town during the course of the 14th century and therefore this setback induced the Florentines to construct a new powerful defensive system. After at first resisting the attempts to capture it by the Aragonesi led by the Duke of Calabria, it finally fell in 1478 after a seige led jointly by the Sienese and by Alfonso d'Aragona.

In Castellina today, we can stil find ample traces of its stormy Medieval past: the urban elliptical structure set around the fortress, the remains of the walls and trenches all testify the inequivocable military origins of the village .

The imposing outline of the **Fortress**, the *Castellina* of long ago which is probably the source of the present place name, with its imposing embattled bastions dominates the local scenery and can clearly be seen from far away. The building, which was restored in the 1930's is dominated by a high keep and is the seat of the Town Council.

Nearby stands the **Parish Church of S. Salvatore** which was reconstructed not long ago, on the site of the original parish building, once forming part of the rectorate of St. Leonino in Conio. The church, which has a beautiful bell-tower alongside it, is built in the Romanesque style and contains a frescoe entitled *Madonna and Child* , done by Lorenzo di Bicci.

The nearby **Via delle Volte** gives us intensely Medieval characteristics. The covered passageways, the arches and the robust walls are tangible proof of the powerful defensive structures of the Florentines.

On the top of a panoramic hill one can visit a vast **Etruscan tomb** (tumulus) which dates back to the 6th century B.C. It was discovered during the 16th century and together with interesting findings which have come to light it proves the existance of ancient Etruscan settlements in the district.

Panorama of Castellina in Chianti (below); on the opposite page: the Parish Church of S. Salvatore.

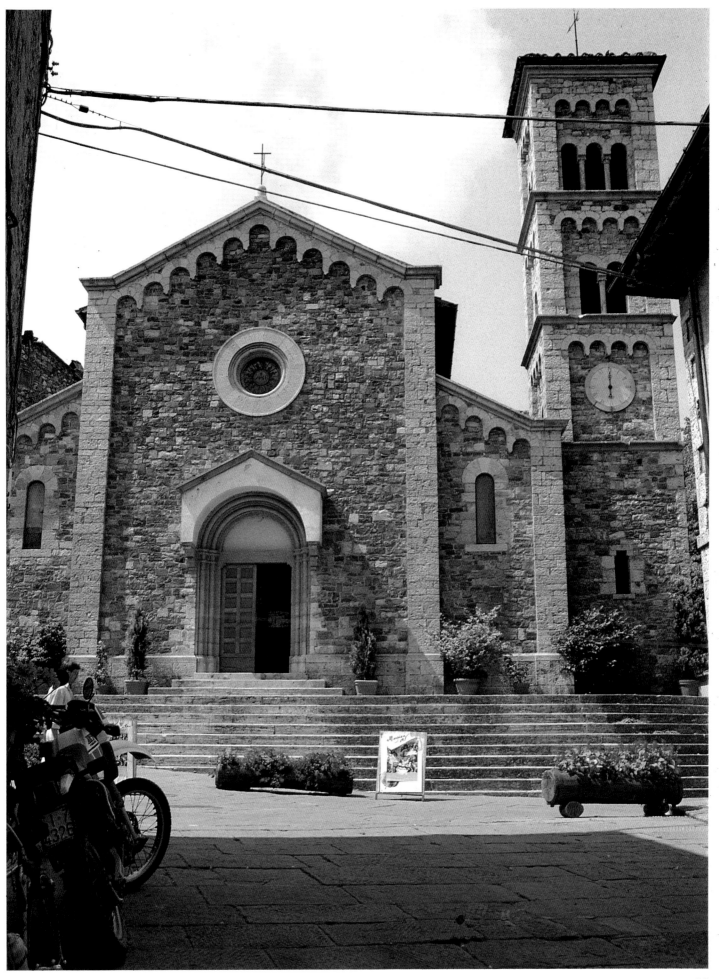

Castellina in Chianti, some enchanting views of the Fortress can be seen in photographs 1, 2 and 6; 3. An Etruscan tomb (6th century B.C.); 4. A view of the characteristic Via delle Volte; 5. A view of Fonterutoli; 7. Vines near Castellina in Chianti.

On the previous pages: a view of the park of the Villa Cerna, 1. Villa Cerna; 2. The ancient oratory in the park of the Villa Cerna; 3. Olive groves near Topina; 4. Rencine, the Church of S. Michele; 5. A view of the luxuriant flora of the Chianti region; 6. Vines in the area where the Chianti Classico is produced.

Recommended excursions in the vicinity

Rencine, this evocative Chianti village is made up by a group of rural houses which stand on a hill facing the fortified citadel of Monteriggioni, not far from the train station of Castellina. Here there once stood one of the Florentine outposts in Sienese territory. Already mentioned as far back as the 11th century, the castle was subjected to the vicissitutes of the secular fight between the two cities and it, too, was destroyed in 1478. Today, there remain only scarse fragmentory traces of the powerful **Castle of Rencine**; the tower and some parts of the walls still exist even if they are in a state of ruin and threatened by negligence and complete abandon. Nearby, in the background of a vast courtyard, enclosed by a wall, stands the beautiful Romanesque façade of the **Church of S. Michele** (11th century). The front of the building, built of square hewn stones is decorated with a sequence of small blind arches.

Cerna, the green and fertile hill is situated in a pleasant geographical and environmental position in the territory of Chianti Classico. Dominating its charming slopes, which are densely covered with vines, stands, surrounded by a beautiful green park, the **Villa Cerna**, a splendid example of an elegant residence of the Chianti regions. Its imposing appearance and its towers which can be seen on the façade show that it was probably put to military use as an ancient fortified building. Besides, its strategic position, in a decidedly 'delicate' area due to the precarious equilibrium caused by the fighting between the Florentines and the Sienese reveals the fundamental necessity of possessing this stronghold. As far back as the 11th century reference has been made to a *Church of S. Donato in Cesarea* at Cerna, in acts which concern the Badia a Isole. In 1203 the villa at Cerna was mentioned with regard to the defining of the boundaries controlled by Florence and Siena, whilst in the second half of the 18th century the building was still known to be the possession of the Benedettini of Badia a Isola. Today the villa is the property of a well-known wine azienda; its interiors bear the stamp of Medieval architecture and show the style of the typical residences of Chianti. In the beautiful park can be seen not only ancient buildings such as an *oratory,* but also a modern swimming pool which is used by the guests, showing how the modern world has made its mark on the region.

Fonterutoli, the significance of this delightful hilly village, situated to the south of the communal chief town, lies in its typical urban structure which clearly shows the signs of the ancient Medieval plan. It was inhabited as far back as Etruscan times and then by the Romans and then played a part in the Medieval conflicts between Florence and Siena. It was, in fact, at Fonterutoli during the course of the 8th century that, if not a lasting peace, at least a type of agreement was looked for by the two cities. Today nothing remains

29

3

of the ancient castle and the church of St. Miniato. The **Villa Mazzei** (16th century) belongs to an ancient family, the owners amongst other things of extensive vines in the district which give a particularly important and much appreciated product.

Castle of Grignano, the Medieval hamlet of Grignano stands on a green hill which dominates the valley of Pesa and is dominated by a tower which was once part of the ancient fortified complex. Already mentioned in official documents as far back as the 11th century, it came under the rule of various patrons up until its destruction in the second half of the 15th century at the hands of Neapolitan soldiers who worked for the Duke of Calabria. It was newly erected by the Florentines and was then, throughout the centuries, gradually transformed for rural use. Of the ancient castle nucleus, remains the beautiful **Tower** which has been carefully and accurately restored by the British writer Raymond Flower.

1. A view of the Castle of Rencine; 2. Villa Cerna, evocative views of the interior architecture; 3. The peaceful courtyard facing the parish of Rencine; 4. Villa Cerna, a typical example of the residences to be found in the Chianti region.

4

31

CASTELNUOVO BERARDENGA

The southernmost commune of the Chianti regions, it is only partially included within the area as Chianti Classico and has 5.905 inhabitants. The city has grown up around a hill which dominates the upper portion of the valley along which the Ombrone runs.

The district of Castelnuovo Berardenga was inhabited as far back as Etruscan times (7th century B.C.). Archeological findings have proved that the area was also inhabited in Roman times. The 'suffix' Berardenga dates back to the 9th century and refers to Berardo, one of the sons of Wuinigi di Ranieri, the ambassador to the Emperor Lodovico and governor of Siena and Roselle. At the beginning of the 14th century, the Sienese built a castle (from which the name Castelnuovo of today derives) which was subjected to various vicissitudes during the war against Florence. As a consequence of the Fall of the Sienese Republic, the fortified structures were dismantled and this event also marked the beginning of the relentless decline of the locality.

The **Parish Church of SS. Giusto and Clemente** is characterized by the plain façade preceded by an imposing Neo-classical pronaos and decorated by powerful columns which sustain a triangular tympanum. On the left side of the building, stands a delightful bell-tower. The interior holds a canvas of exquisite workmanship, painted in 1426 by Giovanni di Paolo which portrays a splendid *Madonna with Child and Angels*. This element was part of a polyptych which was dismantled and transferred in part to the picture gallery of Siena and in part to foreign art galleries and museums.

The **Villa Chigi**, surrounded by a lush and vast park in which we can find centennial plants was constructed at the beginning of the 19th century on the site of a former fortified structure. The villa belongs to the Count Guido Saracini who promoted musical activities here. Today the building is the property of the *'Fondazione Accademia Musicale Chigiana'*.

The scanty remains of a **tower** are all that are left of the ancient 14th century castle. This castle constituted part of the perimeter walls of the fortification and is partly hidden by the dwellings which are grouped together in the higher parts of the locality.

On the opposite page: an enchanting view of the Tower of Grignano; 1. Castelnuovo Berardenga, the Parish Church of S.S. Giusto and Clemente; 2. Castelnuovo Berardenga, Villa Chigi.

1. *Castelnuovo Berardenga, the Town Hall Building; 2. Castelnuovo Berardenga, one of the typical lanes in the historic centre; 3. Castelnuovo Berardenga; the Madonna with child and Angels (16the century) in the Parish Church of S.S. Giusto and Clemente; 4. S. Gusmè,. a view of the medieval village.*

S. Gusmè, the Town Gate.

The apse of the Church of S.S. Cosma and Damiano.

Recommended excursions in the vicinity

San Gusmè, this beautiful village can reasonably be defined as one of the pearls of the district of Berardenga. Situated in a magnificent environmental position, a little further on from the turning for Brolio, it is set in a spot rendered all the more evocative thanks to the Medieval lay-out which has come down to us through the centuries still intact. The ancient walls, the gates, the narrow lanes and the arches all make up the indelible reminder of the past, which seems to come to life in this corner of the Sienese land, miraculously conserved even to the present day. Already mentioned as far back as the 19th century, the **Church of SS. Cosma and Damiano**, from which the place name, San Gusmè is derived, is a little jewel of Romanesque architecture. The façade, in elegant blocks of square stone, stands alongside the walls where the civic gates can be seen. The apse, decorated by slender mullioned windows is surmounted by a graceful bell-tower. As regards the town gates, particularly interesting due to the architectonic elements and the setting in which they are to be found, the Northern gate is surmounted by the characteristic Sienese coat of arms with its two-coloured black and white band, and the gate in the Southern part of the wall, where the arch in serein stone surmounted by an effigy of the *Madonna and Child* can be seen.

Montaperti, the locality is famous for the epic battle which took place here on the 4th of September 1260 between the armies of Florence and Siena. The small pyramidal 'cippus' (boundary stone), to be found on a hill shaded by the foilage of the cypresses, is the only testimony of the famous battle rendered immortal by the verses of Dante Alighieri ('the torture and the slaughter which coloured the Arbia red').

Charterhouse of Pontignano, this monastic complex, which today is the seat of the college of the University of Siena, was constructed in the first half of the 14th century, and was enlarged during the 15th century. In the ancient refectory one can admire the '*Last Supper*', a fresco by Bernardino Poccetti.

35

GAIOLE IN CHIANTI

The commune of Gaiole in Chianti has 2.580 inhabitants and lies in a woody area on the slopes of the so-called Mountains of Chianti, along the road which joins the Chianti regions with Valdarno (Arezzo). The Gaiole of today, which is crossed by the Massellone river, does not possess any major tourist attractions, except for some Medieval buildings and a stone tower which was once perhaps an ancient mill. Nonetheless its neighbouring district is so full of parish churches, castles and Medieval hamlets that it makes up a necessary stop on any tourist itinerary of the Chianti regions.

The origins of the place-name of Gaiole seem to go back to a Longobard term, from which the word *gagiolum* is derived, signifying a wood which could be reached by the herds and which was rich in pasture land. An important market place as far back as Medieval times (11th century) Gaiole has always continued to develop its role as a commercial and transport centre for the nearby Badia a Coltibuono and the castles of Meleto, Vertine and Barbischio. Once the seat of a tertiary of the League of Chianti (13th century), it, too, was subjected to the endemic counterblows of the Medieval conflicts.

The **Church of S. Sigismondo**, alongside which can be found a slender bell-tower, brightened up by mullioned windows is a modern building obviously inspired by the Gothic style.

Recommended excursions in the vicinity

Spaltenna, the sight of this exceptional Medieval complex can already be seen from the road at the bottom of the valley which leads to Gaiole. On the summit of a green hill, covered by rows of vines and crowned by the characteristic outline of the cypress trees, stands the imposing turreted façade of the **Castle of Spaltenna**, behind which stands out the square outline of the bell-tower of the parish which bears the same name. Once a convent, already mentioned in the 12th century, it is used today as a hotel and gives a clear example of the numerous transformations of ancient buildings in the Chianti area due to tourism. These have almost a dual role in that they reveal a love for the past but yet show how the modern way of life (farmhouse holidays, for example) has become part of the area. The nearby **Parish Church of Spaltenna** is an ancient Romanesque place of worship. Already known in the 11th century as *San Pietro in Avenano*, it was thereafter dedicated to *St. Mary*. The building, which is divided into three parts in the interior, has been given back its ancient splendour by restoration work which, thankfully, has eliminated the more unfortunate 18th century additions, now showing clearly the simplicity and the beauty of its limestone walls.

On the opposite page: S. Gusmè, a detail of the Town Gate with the coat of arms of Siena; 1. Spaltenna Castle; 2. A view of Gaiole in Chianti; 3. Spaltenna Castle, the interior courtyard.

Vertine, amongst the numerous villages set high up in the district of Gaiole, Vertine is the one which offers landscape characteristics and environmental elements which are difficult to find elsewhere. Once known as *Vertinulae* in acts of the 10th century, it was afterwards controlled by Badia di Coltibuono. It then became the possession of the Florentines, and was always on the sidelines of the bitter contests which raged throughout the Medieval period in the Chianti area. Perhaps due to this fact, it has been able to maintain its structural entirety and its unparalleled Medieval lay-out, which has been handed down to us in an excellent state of repair. A visit to this little centre permits the tourist to see how Man has contributed to the architecture of the place with its narrow streets that have centennial houses built from great blocks of square stone rising up on either side. The visible remains of the walls, the imposing and elevated **Keep**, which seems to guard the entrance of a nearby town gate, the quiet small piazza, onto which faces the beautiful façade of the **Church of S. Pietro** (in the interior we find works by Lorenzo di Bicci and Duccio di Buoninsegna) evoke tangible Medieval suggestions.

S. Donato in Perano, the locality has origins which date back to the 10th century; during that time the place had a castle, which today no longer exists. It was purchased by the Florentine family, the Strozzi in the 16th century. San Donato in Perano was then transformed into a sumptuous 17th century country residence. Due to the restructuring work the castle disappeared and the church bearing the same name was transformed into a chapel. Today the **Villa of S. Donato in Perano** bears the signs of recent restoration work which has given back to the building the elegance of its architectonic lines and the beauty of its decorative elements.

Villa di Vistarenni, the unmistakable and harmonious façade of this beautiful 17th century villa is clearly visible from the road which goes from Radda in Chianti to Gaiole. We find reference to *Fistarinne* in official acts of the 11th century; at that period, in this locality, stood an ancient village. The construction, as we see it today, has two flights of steps at the entrance, whilst at the top of the central portion of the façade a decorative element of marked Baroque influence stands out. It is worthwhile visiting the cellars as they are carved out of the living rock. The villa dominates a hill which is covered in vines and also has a small chapel which dates back to the 16th century.

Coltibuono Abbey, the magnificent monastic complex is situated at the extremes of the eastern borders of the Chianti region, near the road that leads to Montevarchi. According to tradition the founding of the first abbatial nucleus dates back to the 8th century. However it is known that the Benedictine monks of Vallombrosa lived here, dedicating their lives to rural activities as far back as the 12th century. The completion of the present building was finished between the 15th and the 18th centurias. The suppression of the

On page 38: 1. A view of the farm and the Villa at Vistarenni; 2-3 The Parish Church of Spaltenna with its characteristic square bell-tower; on page 39: an evocative view of the Parish Church and the bell-tower of Spaltenna as seen from the park surrounding the Castle of Spaltenna; on the opposite page: the high Keep of Vertine, situated near the entrance gate to the old village, with decidedly medieval characteristics; a typical view of the ancient town lay-out of Vertine (above).

41

monastery in 1810, in compliance with a Napoleonic edict, meant that the building was abandoned by the monks and was then transformed into an agricultural azienda. The **Abbatial Church**, of exquisite Romanesque form, is dominated by the imposing embattled bell-tower. Behind the main part of the buildings the apse, situated at the end of the nave, juts out.

Barbischio, this enchanting Medieval hamlet is set out along the summit of a hill which dominates the town of Gaiole. The first mention of *Barbistio* goes back to the Medieval period: originally it was a modest settlement, it first fell into the hands of Ricasoli and then passed to the Guidi Counts. It was then once again controlled by the original proprietors and then strengthened by a powerful system of fortifications, which were dismantled in the first half of the 16th century. According to an accredited theory, the founding of Gaiole was originally intended as a market place for Barbischio. Today the typical structure of the place, the ancient houses of clearly Medieval plan, the remains of the **Keep** and the restructured **Tower** have all played a part in handing down through history, the traditions of this proud and ancient village.

Castle of Meleto, the imposing turreted glacices of the Castle of Meleto remind us of its original military use, splendidly conserved in its present form by complete restructuring work carried out in the 18th century. The first mention of this castle dates back to the 12th century when it belonged to the Badia di Coltibuono and to the family of Firidolfi Ricasoli. In the second half of the 15th century, it was partially dismantled by the Sienese and was then reconstructed by the Florentines. It was once again destroyed by the wars which took place in the first half of the 16th century, it was then transformed in the 18th century and became a residence for the gentry. The interiors have extremely interesting motifs as can be seen in the frescoes of the halls and the characteristic little theatre which dates from the 18th century.

Castagnoli, a picturesque rural hamlet which dominates a scenic hill, it captures the eye thanks to its landscape and environmental qualities. Already mentioned in the 11th century, as the territory of the noblemen of Berardenga, it was then aquired by the abbots of Coltibuono, before passing into the hands of Ricasoli. Its castle was at the centre of the attempts to conquer the territory during the wars, which, in the 15th - 16th centuries took place in the Chianti region. The massive outline of the **Castle** is still today in an excellent state of repair, and can be seen surrounded by numerous rural dwellings.

1. Vertine, the beautiful façade of the Church of S. Pietro; 2. A detail of the Villa of S. Donato in Perano; 3. A view of the rural village of Rietine; 4. Castagnoli, a view of the imposing castle.

3

4

1

2

3

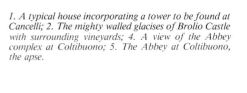

1. A typical house incorporating a tower to be found at Cancelli; 2. The mighty walled glacises of Brolio Castle with surrounding vineyards; 4. A view of the Abbey complex at Coltibuono; 5. The Abbey at Coltibuono, the apse.

4

5

Castle of Brolio, probably the most illustrious of the castles in the Chianti area, it stands in a scenic position at the top of a hill which is densely covered with vines and olive groves, and dominates the valley of Arbia. It belonged, as far back as the 11th century, to the Ricasoli family, and it was a formidable stronghold in a strategic position at the boundaries of the Florentine lands, alternatively occupied by the Florentines and the Sienese. Dismantled by the Aragones in 1478, it returned to the Florentines, who then reconstructed it, from 1484 onwards. This reconstruction made it into one of the first fortresses to be fortified with ramparts in Italy. The castle was protected by the solid town walls, which have an irregular pentagonal plan and a perimeter of 450 mts. These are thought to be amongst the first fortified works of Giuliano da Sangallo. Inside the building is the **Chapel of S. Jacopo** with a polyptych by a painter in the style of Ugolino di Nerio, known by the name of the Maestro of Brolio, and some mosaics, designed by Alessandro Franchi. We can also see the **Keep** fortified by towers (greatly restored). At the side of the latter is the main palace which was almost completely rebuilt in the Neo-gothic style in 1860 by Pietro Marchetti, with a large dining-hall decorated with Flemish tapestries. The castle is connected to the fame of the illustrious political man Bettino Ricasoli (Florence 1809 - Brolio 1880), the so-called 'Iron Baron' who lived here for a long time promoting the famous wine production of the surrounding countryside.

Lecchi, this tranquil rural hamlet is situated on the road to Radda in Chianti. Nearby, at the top of a hill, which is brightened up by the green foilage of the cypresses, stands the restored tower of the ancient **Castle of Monteluco a Lecchi**. Already mentioned in acts dating back to the 10th century, it became the property of Ricasoli, then passing under the control of the Florentines in the second half of the 12th century. Repeatedly subjected to destruction during the wars of the Medieval period, it started to fall into decline in the first half of the 16th century. A little beneath the castle, stands the delightful small Romanesque church of **S. Martino**.

45

S. Polo in Rosso, the characteristic turreted complex stands in an extremely enchanting position, dominating the valley along which the Arbia river runs. The building complex, as seen today, makes up a Parish, thanks to the transformations carried out through the centuries. This **parish**, of probable palaneo-Christian origins, is first mentioned in acts concerning Badia di Coldibuono as far back as the 11th century. Due to its favourable strategic position, during the wars in the Chianti regions, it was fortified as far back as the 8th century, finally coming under the control of the Sienese (1478). Once more controlled by the Florentines, it started to fall into decline with the downfall of the Sienese Republic. The church, which has been restructured has a pleasant Romanesque design. The interior, divided into three parts, contains some Gothic designs and has a cycle of religiously-inspired frescos (14th century).

1. The Castle of Monteluco at Lecchi, an important example of the modern restructuring work carried out on the ancient turreted structure; 2. A view of Barbischio, a typical hilltop village to be found in the verdant Chianti region; 3. The imposing fortified structure of the Castle of Meleto; 4. A view of the Castle of S. Polo in Rosso; 5. The warm tonalities of the morning sunshine highlight the splendid architectonic features of the Castle of Meleto.

47

GREVE IN CHIANTI

The chief town of the so-called Florentine Chianti numbers 11.013 inhabitants and is situated in the heart of the Classic Chianti region on the banks of the river of the same name. All around stretches a countryside made up of pleasant fertile hills, while the parishes, hamlets and numerous castles represent the more tangible aspects of man's ancient exploitation of these lands.

The first mention of the place dates back to XI century documents and it seems certain that the locality grew up along an important road leading to Florence, as the market place for the nearby hill village of Montefioralle. Regarding the existence of a castle at Greve, it is known for certain that it was destroyed by Alberico da Barbiano in the second half of the XIV century. Greve in Chianti is also known for having been the cradle of the share system and still today offers a family-type organization in rural activities, although with the innovations and transformations introduced by modern technology.

The locality, well-known for its annual *Exhibition Market of Classic Chianti*, is set out around the beautiful spacious **Piazza Matteotti** which reveals, in its terraced porticoes and in the vastity of its dimensions, its ancient function as a market place. In the square there is also the *monument to Giovanni da Verrazzano*.

The scenic effect of the square is completed by the front of the **Parish Church of S. Croce (The Holy Cross)** which tends towards the classic style. The rebuilding of this church, inspired by neoclassic criteria, dates from the first half of the XIX century. In its interior can be seen an *Annunciation of the Virgin Mary* carried out by Bicci di Lorenzo and a *Virgin Mary and Saints* attributed to the Master of Greve (Maestro di Greve).

S. Francis' Oratory is all that remains of an ancient complex belonging to a convent suppressed in the last century; in its interior a *Deposition* by the Blind Man of Gambassi (Cieco di Gambassi) is conserved together with a terracotta work from the workshop of Della Robbia.

1. The beautiful, spacious Piazza Matteotti has always been the pulsing heart of the chief town of the Florentine Chianti; 2. The Palazzo Municipale acts as a background to the monument to Giovanni di Verrazzano; on on the following page: a characteristic many-towered building in the centre of Greve in Chianti.

1. A detail of Piazza Matteotti with the monument to Giovanni da Verrazzano; 2. Festival day at Lucolena di Greve; 3. A clay sculpture in the Parish Church of S. Croce at Greve in Chianti; on the opposite page: a typical shop selling cold-cuts under the porticoes of Piazza Matteotti.

Recommended Excursions in the Vicinity

Montefioralle, the locality is made up of one of the most typical ancient villages of the Chianti territory. Of particular interest are the urbanisation typologies which reveal a clear medieval matrix. The remains of the old walls, the houses in blocks of squared stone and the precious flagging which paves the narrow lanes represent points of great interest for the visitor. Once named *Monteficalle*, it was not spared from destruction following fierce medieval conflicts, even though it could count on enviable fortifications. Montefioralle is the place where the Vespucci family originated, the family of the famous navigator Amerigo, and it is the centre which has determined the rise and development of the nearby Greve. At the highest point of the medieval aggregate arises **St. Stephen's Church**, inside which can be admired paintings from the XIII - XV centuries.

1. Montefioralle, the pretty façade of St. Stephen's Church; 2. A narrow alley paved with stone recalls the medieval atmosphere of an ancient district at Montefioralle; on the following page: a typical view of the medieval design of Montefioralle.

1

2

Panzano, this centre which has extremely ancient origins is situated along a rolling spur of hillside which overlooks an extensive panorama. There once existed here a rural Roman village known as *Flaccianus*. Mentioned as being a castle as far back as the XII century, Panzano was part of the Greve League, being involved in the bloody wars between Florence and Siena. The lofty **Keep** is the most notable testimony of the ancient castle structure, around which huddles the medieval village. Part of the ancient walls and some bracketed towers still enable one to locate the original periphery of the fortifications. The **Church of St. Mary**, still to be seen, is a result of work carried out on the original 13th century installation during the last century; it is flanked by a tower which was part of an ancient defence system.

1. A view of the Church of St. Mary flanked by its ancient bell-tower; 2. An angle of the ancient Castle of Panzano dominated by the tall structure of its Keep; on the following page: a view of the village of Panzano overshadowed by the Keep and the Church of St. Mary.

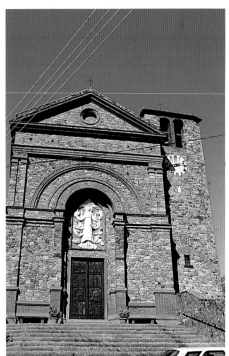

Parish Church of S. Leolino, despite the 18th century aspect given to it by the portico in front of the façade, the parish church has much older origins, possibly older than its first mention in the X century. The interior of the building, scanned by three naves, follows the pattern of the Roman parish churches and can be related to the XII century. Among the numerous works of art brought to light during restoration work at the beginning of the 1940's one should mention a *Christ's Baptism* ascribed to pupils of Ghirlandaio, a triptych carried out by Mariotto di Nardo, an alterpiece believed to be the work of Berlinghieri (XIII century) and a triptych carried out by the Master of Panzano (Maestro di Panzano). Near to the building is a charming XIV century cloister.

Colognole, characteristic rural aggregate, it is situated in a pleasant sunny position, dominating a cultivated hillock which slopes down to the Greve valley. A heavy squared tower, which rises between the buildings heralds the so-called **Castle of Colognole**. The origins of this construction are uncertain and it is distinguished by the impressiveness which the huge blocks give to it. It is certain that it was razed to the ground in the second half of the XII century, and that it has reached us by way of a series of restructural modifications and enlargements.

1

2

56

Verrazzano Castle, a delightful tower topped by battlements hails from afar the complex of buildings (many of which have a marked modern imprint) grouped around the original manor house. Today the building has the air of an elegant gentleman's dwelling and conserves scant traces of the primitive structure. Its notoriety is due to the fact that it was once the residence of the Da Verrazzano, the noble Florentine family to which belonged Giovanni who, in the first half of the XVI century explored vast portions of the Canadian and North American coastline on behalf of Francis I of France.

Vicchiomaggio Castle, the central nucleus of the building is situated in a particularly pleasant position, surrounded by green cypress trees overlooking the Greve valley. Mention of it is made in the X century as *Vicchio dei Lombardi*, and its origins are founded in the Longobard era. From the XVI century the castle and its small village assume their present denomination which calls to mind the popular feast days of the Calendimaggio, very common in Florence at that time. The castle of Vicchiomaggio in all probability received Leonardo da Vinci who included it in some of his papers. The building as it stands today has a composite structure since elements of clearly medieval stamp, such as the charming battlemented covered tower, co-exist with aspects which are evidence of the re-conversion to a country villa in the XVII century.

Mugnana, this locality high up in the Ema valley presents rural and architectural interests of a notable level. Here the Chianti hills become more mountainous and wooded. Towards the east they are delineated by the spurs of the Scalari mountains which separate them from the actual Valdarno. In this geographical context, separated by the Rio di Sezzate (Sezzate stream) rise up on two hillocks the Castles of Mugnana and Sezzate which still seem to oppose one another, perpetuating the memory of ancient medieval battles. The **Castle of Mugnana** has been known of since the XI century. Towards the end of the XII century a pact was ratified here which founded the Chianti League. Particularly worthy of note are the majestic stone tower and the lovely XIV century arcaded courtyard. The **Castle of Sezzate** reminds one of a painting with marked medieval connotations; mentioned as far back as the XII century it has recently been restored to its original aspect. Around the mighty walls on the crest of the hill stretch the ancient houses and rustic hamlets.

1. A view of Verrazzano Castle, once residence of the noble Florentine family; 2. The porticoed façade of the Parish Church of S. Leolino; opposite: an evocative view of the Castle of Sezzate with its cluster of rustic houses.

1

2

59

3

4

On page 58: The Parish Church of S. Leolino, "The Baptism of Christ" work of pupils of Ghirlandaio and the baptismal font; on page 59: 1. Our Lady with Saints Catherine, Peter and Paul, a valuable triptych believed to be the work of the Maestro di Greve (XIII century); 2. The Virgin and Child between Saints Peter and Paul, an altarpiece believed to be the work of Meliore di Jacopo (XIII century); on the opposite page: 1. An angle of the Castle of Colognole; 2. A farm in the Comune of Greve in Chianti; 3. A view of the many-towered Vicchiomaggio Castle; 4. The delightful façade of the Chiesa di S. Tommaso at Giobbole faces onto the road which connects Greve to Florence.

POGGIBONSI

This important town, numbering 26.553 inhabitants, is situated at the foot of the Chianti hills at an important arterial junction. The Poggibonsi of our time possesses an active industrial sector, flanked by a dynamic services sector and traditional rural activities. Its municipal territory includes a very small portion of the Classic Chianti and the town, excluding its more ancient core, has a substantially modern stamp.

The place however has quite remote origins; from the second half of the XIII century it was known as *Borgo Marturi* (*Marturi Village*). Subsequently it took the present name which is a derivation of *Poggiobonizio*, the castle (*Podium Bonitii*) razed to the ground by Guido di Monforte at the time of the medieval contests. Passed into the hands of the Florentines, it was further strengthened with fortifications.

The urbanistici fabric of most ancient date grew up around **Palazzo Pretorio (Magistrate's Palace)**. The façade of this building, which has clearly gothic connotations, is decorated with numerous coats of arms and is flanked by an ancient battlemented tower.

The nearby **Collegiata (Collegiate Church)** is the 19th century reconstruction of an ancient place of worship which utilises the tower (still standing) of the Poggio Marturi as a belltower. In the interior one can admire a 14th century marble baptismal font and a *Resurrection* by Vincenzo Tamagni.

The 14th century **Church of St. Lorenzo** was almost entirely recontructured after World War II. In the apsidal portion is the art work of major worth; a valuable wooden *Crucifix* by Giovanni d'Agostino (XIV century).

On page 62: the evocative Castle of Mugnana rises above the thick vegetation of the Chianti region; on page 63: a view of the majestic stone tower of the Castle of Mugnana; 1. Poggibonsi, the Collegiate Church; 2. Poggibonsi, Magistrate's Palace; 3. A view over Poggibonsi dominated by the Abbey Castle.

Recommended Excursions in the Vicinity

S. Lucchese, close to the town of Poggibonsi in a pleasant panoramic setting is the **Basilica of St. Lucchese**. The present edifice is the product of transformations carried out on the original place of worship of the Camaldolesi. Passed to the Franciscans in the first half of the XIII century, alterations and additions turned it into an interesting conventual complex. The interior houses works of high artistic value amongst which should be pointed out several frescoes by Bartolo di Fredi (XIV century), a *Miracle of St. Lucchese* by an unknown 14th century artist and an alterpiece in the style of Della Robbia (XVI century). A *refectory* opens onto the internal **cloister** which houses the masterpiece of Geri-

no da Pistoia: a 16th century affresco representing the *Multiplication of the Bread*. In the area we also find the 13th century **Fairies' Fountain**, architecturally of great worth, and the mighty ramparts which form the remains of the 15th century **Fortezza di Poggio Imperiale (Imperial Hill Fortress)**. The impressive fortification was commissioned by the Medici family from Giuliano da Sangallo, but was never completed.

Castello di Badia (Abbey Castle), the splendid battlemented complex, result of a radical reconstruction project concluded in the second half of the last century, arises from a panoramic hill which dominates Poggibonsi. Mentioned in deeds belonging to the Marquisate of Tuscany at the end of the 10th century, it was subsequently acquired by the Benedictine Monks who turned it into a convent.

Staggia, this tranquil fraction of the Poggibonsi Commune represents one of the happiest examples of medieval military architecture. Mentioned as far back as the X century, Staggia carried out a decisive role throughout the Middle Ages. Fortified several times by the Sienese and Florentines, it was famous for being impregnable. The **Rocca (Citadel)** is the most interesting of the ancient fortresses; a 15th century battlemented Keep dominates the walls, largely in ruin, in which are set several lookout towers. The **Parish Church of St. Mary of the Assumption (S. Maria Assunta)** has been considerably altered by restoration work and rebuilding which have changed the original 13th century design. In the interior one can admire some valuable paintings, bits of XIV century affrescoes and a 15th century window with a effigy of *Mary Magdalen*.

Strozzavolpe Castle, the unmistakable battlemented profile of this castle rises up from the summit of a hill enriched by the green foliage of cypress trees. Its position overlooking the Imperial Hill Fortress supports the hypothesis that it was an advance bulwark in the complex system of fortifications for the nearby Podium Bonitii. Particularly suggestive is the high tower crowned by battlements and enriched by a delightful little balcony over the entrance arch.

Talciona Parish Church, this church, dedicated to *Our Lady of the Assumption*, is situated on the side of the road which runs through the quiet rural village of Talciona. The building, in a most charming Roman style (XII century) has a particularly interesting façade where a sculpture portraying the *Adoration of the Magi* (XIII century) and a large ornate eye stand out.

Parish Church of St. Peter at Cedda, the delightful Roman church dates back to the XII century. The absidal portion is particularly suggestive flanked by a robust square belltower and embellished by a sequence of suspended blind arches. Both the inside and the outside offer a large number of Roman sculptured motives, portraying the ancient Christian symbols, heads, and human and animalesque figures. The interior houses a *Virgin Mary with Saints* of Florentine impression.

On page 66: Basilica of St. Lucchese, Virgin with Child and Saints, altarpiece in the style of the Della Robbia family; on page 67: 1. A view of the Basilica of St. Lucchese; 2. Basilica of St. Lucchese, the 14th-century frescoes; 3. Staggia, a view of the Rocca; 4. Staggia, The Parish Church of St. Mary of the Assumption.

3

4

4

5

1. An evocative view from the Chianti hills towards Luco and the Strozzavolpe Castle; 2. A lovely crenellated tower at the entrance to the Strozzavolpe Castle; 3. Strozzavolpe Castle, the internal building; 4. Luco seen from the Strozzavolpe Castle; 5. Staggia, an angle of the medieval town walls.

3

4

1. *The warm tones bestowed by the sunset light up the lovely Romanesque façade of the Parish Church of St. Peter at Cedda; 2. Talciona Parish Church, a detail of the frieze over the doorway (Adoration of the Magi, XIII century); 3. A panorama of the vineyards with the Fortress of Poggio Imperiale in the background; 4. A view of the medieval Talciona Parish Church.*

RADDA IN CHIANTI

The Commune of Radda in Chianti numbers 1.597 inhabitants. The pleasant centre stands on the summit of a hilly ridge which separates the Valley of Pesa from that of Arbia. The urban topography of Radda faithfully reflects the evolution of a small medieval centre, still contained within the confines of its walls, with the narrow streets paved in stone and the lovely façades of old palaces. Mentioned in documents from the XI century it ended up gravitating to the Florentine sphere of influence (Lodo di Poggibonsi 1203). In spite of being reinforced with the addition of fortifications, it suffered notable inconvenience throughout the Middle Ages, when it also carried out administrative functions as seat of one of the service sectors of the Chianti League.

Radda has conserved almost unaltered its aspects of a medieval environment, with ample portions of the ancient walls against which lean the characteristic Chianti-style dwellings. The **Palazzo Pretorio (Magistrate's Palace)**, actual municipal seat, is a pleasant 15th century building with two arches on the ground floor and embellished with a good number of mayoral coats of arms, amongst which can be noted that of Francesco Ferrucci.

On the opposite side a flight of steps embellished with a lovely fountain leads to the **Chiesa di S. Nicolò (St. Nicholas's Church)**. The building has a gothic front adorned by an affresco and flanked by a battlemented belltower, a faithful reconstruction, completed in the 1920's, of a type of belltower widely found throughout the Chianti territory. Inside, also modern, is conserved a lovely wooden XV century *Crucifix*.

The **Chiesa dei Francescani (Franciscans' Church)** is enriched by a pleasant portico which winds along the front. This building is part of a conventual complex erected by the monks, who established themselves in the place from the beginning of the development and expansion of their Order in the Chianti territory.

1. Radda in Chianti, the bell-tower of the Parish Church; 2. Numerous mayoral coats of arms decorate the pleasing façade of the Magistrate's Palace at Radda.

1. Panorama over Radda in Chianti; 2. Church and Convent of S. Francesco; 3. The façade of the Church of S. Nicolò; 4. The Church of S. Nicolò, the 15th-century wooden Crucifix.

3

2

4

1

3

2

76

Recommended Excursions in the Vicinity

Volpaia, typical hillside centre on the eastern spurs of the Chianti mountains, the locality dominates the underlying Pesa valley. Strategically important from the X century the medieval nucleus of Volpaia developed along the demarcation line between contrasting interests on the part of Florentines and Sienese. Mentioned in documents as far back as the XII century it eventually became part of the Florentine possessions and for this reason often suffered disastrous counterblows in the centuries-old hostilities between the two cities. In the second half of the XV century the Castle of Volpaia was subjected to joint Sienese and Aragonese sieges. The decline of the place was started by the irreversible deterioration of the Sienese Republic in the XVI century. Volpaia has maintained the salient features of medieval town planning and offers aspects of stimulating ambiental and landscape interest. The narrow paved alleys and the robust houses made out of sandstone make up the salient notes in a piece of the Middle Ages which has been passed down to us. A high **Keep** dominates the charming square which greets the visitor; it is all that remains of the ancient castle. Not far away, in a quiet square adorned with the suggestive parapet of a well, is the simple linear front of the **Commenda di S. Eufrosino**. The building, no longer in use, was realised in the XV century and recalls motives of obvious Brunelleschian inspiration.

Monterinaldi Castle, its presence looms from high up on a hill which overlooks the bed of the river Pesa and the parallel road that runs through the valley bottom. It would seem that the first human settlements in the area had their roots in Etruscan age. In the early Middle Ages Monterinaldi was the property of the Longobard count Gottifredo and subsequently given in feud to the Guidi counts. The locality was spared the conflicts which tormented these Chianti regions. Towards the middle of the XII century the Florentines suffered a hard defeat here at the hands of the Sienese. Of the original castle there remain scarce traces; the entire complex has been transformed over the centuries and in the 1960's it underwent conspicuous conservation work.

4

1. Radda in Chianti, a characteristic street in the town centre; 2. Radda in Chianti, view of the walls and medieval buildings; 3. Volpaia, the Commenda di S. Eufrosino; 4. Volpaia Castle; 5. The crenellated tower of Monterinaldi rises above the village's rustic houses.

5

SAN CASCIANO VAL DI PESA

The locality, which numbers 15.679 inhabitants, is situated in the north of the Chianti region, on a ridge of hills that divides the Pesa valley from the Greve valley. At San Casciano important roads branch out and the town as a whole preserves its individual character, set apart from the other Chianti towns. San Casciano Val di Pesa has markedly urban connotations although decidedly medieval corners, or churches and buildings of architectural and artistic interest are to be found.

It is thought that the locality was known as far back as the Roman era at which time it was an important station on the consular Cassia road. During the Middle Ages it was subjected to the Florentine bishops, finally becoming a stronghold of the Florentine Republic. In the first half of the XIV century San Casciano suffered from the war which Castruccio Castracani conducted under its walls. At the time of the short-lived government of Florence by the Duke of Athens a massive defence settlement was undertaken, finally completed by the Florentine rulers in 1356. In the Medici era Cosimo the First further strengthened the fortifications, the importance of which gradually lessened after the fall of the Sienese Republic.

Today some very well-preserved tracts of the **walls**, a tower and scarce traces of the castle give testimony to the medieval past of this spot.

Particularly worthy of note is what is left of the **Keep** of the ancient fortifications. Nowadays it is lost in the greenery of a garden which belongs to an elegant private residence. Its imposing aspect, the two blind arches turned towards the portal and the tops of the elegant Ghibelline battlements have recently been restored to their original splendour by a most satisfactory renovation.

4

5

1. A corner of Monterinaldi, characteristic hill village above the Pesa valley; 2. Volpaia, a characteristic coat of arms in majolica; 3. A glimpse of the medieval village of Volpaia; 4. San Casciano Val di Pesa, the Keep; 5. San Casciano Val di Pesa, a typical aspect of the ancient centre.

The **Chiesa della Misericordia (Church of Charity)** is situated close to the door which is set into the ancient walls. In olden times the church was known as *S. Maria del Prato* (*S. Mary on the Green*) and this name clearly referred to its surroundings before the urban boundaries were realised. This 14th century building presents typical Tuscan-gothic characteristics and was patched up in the XVI century. Its interior is of exceptional artistic significance because of the large amount of works housed in it. We would mention a pulpit enriched by bas-relief work carried out by Giovanni di Balduccio, a very noteworthy *Crucifix* in wood dating from the XV century, believed to be the work of pupils of Donatello, a *Circumcision* by Jacopo Vignali, an *Our Lady of the Rosary* by Matteo Martelli, parts of a triptych by Ugolino di Neri, works by Taddeo Gaddi and a valuable *Virgin Mary with Child and Saints*, probably by Bartolomeo della Porta.

The **Chiesa del Suffragio (Church of the Suffrages)** originally a hospice for the Franciscans of the Observants, it was transformed into the Monastery of St. Clare at the turn of the XV century. From the first half of the XIX century the meetings of the *Compagnia del Suffragio* were held here and these meetings still take place today. Newly consecrated in 1952, after reconstruction made necessary by war damage, it has recently been turned into a museum.

The **Museo di Arte Sacra (Museum of Sacred Works)** finds its well-deserved place in the *Church of the Suffrages* (or *S. Maria del Gesù*). The idea of grouping in this place of worship the various works collected from numerous churches in the district in order to keep them safe from theft and carelessness has led to a collection of extremely interesting medieval religious works of art.

A large quantity of valuable jewelry, furnishings, goldrolled bronzed astylar crosses, chalices, ostensorium, XIV century *Madonnas*, Renaissance fabrics and cloth, make up the basic elements of this worthy initiative. Among the works of art of major importance are works by Francesco Fiorentino, Cenni di Francesco, Jacopo del Casentino, Neri di Bicci, Pier Dandini, Gino Micheli, Maestro di Cabestany.

The 18th century **Collegiata (Collegiate Church)** houses the *Annunciation* painted by artists from Ghirlandaio's workshop and a lovely baptismal font in the lunette of which is portrayed a *Virgin Mary and Saints*, work of the XIV century Florentines.

On the opposite page: The Church of the Suffrages houses the interesting Museum of Sacred Works; 1. Church of the Suffrages, Virgin and Child (Lippo di Benivieni); 2. San Casciano Val di Pesa, an old city doorway.

3

2

On the apposite page: The Church of Charity (S. Maria del Prato); Museum of Sacred Works, 1. Polychrome wooden angel (XVII century); 2. Virgin with Child (Jacopo del Casentino); 3. Liturgical abjects and sculptures by Della Robbia; 4. Coronation of the Virgin (Neri di Bicci).

4

1. San Casciano Val di Pesa, liturgical objects from the XVI-XVII centuries; 2. Astylar, crucifixes from the XIII century; 3. Triptych by Maestro di S. Jacopo at Mucciana; 4. Stele from a XII century baptismal font; 5. Virgin with Child, valuable wooden XIII century sculpture originally in the Parish Church at Castelbonsi.

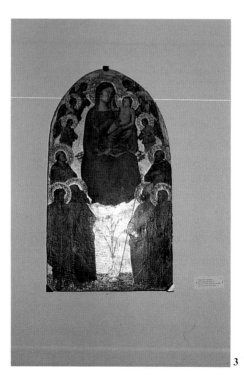

1. San Casciano Val di Pesa; Museo di Arte Sacra, the beautiful wooden Crucifix by Maestro di S. Lucchese; 2. Virgin with Child (XIV century); 3. Virgin with Child and Angels (Francesco Fiorentino); 4. Virgin with Child (Cenni di Francesco Cenni).

Recommended Excursions in the Vicinity

Parish Church of St. Pancras, was founded in the X century on an obviously Roman plan which appears in all its beauty, notwithstanding the addition to the façade of a portico (XVII century). This ancient church is situated on the edge of the built-up area of the same name, on a hill from which can be admired an amazing panorama which reflects the rural countryside so typical of Tuscany. The inside of the building presents a tripartition of the nave and offers enjoyment of the contemplation of a large number of works of art. We would point out a *Virgin Mary with Child and Two St. Johns* by Taddeo Gaddi, a *Christ Crucified and the Marys*, a worthy 16th century painting by Santi di Tito. Several efforts at refurbishing the rectory have brought to light same affrescoed paintings which are believed to be the works of Poccetti.

Castello di Pergolato (Pergolato Castle), the ancient manor house arises in a felicitous position dominating a steep crag which drops down brusquely to the Pesa valley. Its construction dates back to the X century and originally had the aspect of a well-supplied fortress. Despite its brooding appearance it is a decidedly suggestive building. The 18th century reconversion to a residence has made available to us one of the more typical country houses of the Chianti region, characterised by the refined elegance of its interior.

Montefiridolfi, this tranquil rural centre is situated on the fertile hills which lie between the Pesa valley and the course of the Terzona river. At one time the **Montefiridolfi castle**, property of the Buondelmonti family, rose up here. The ancient structure can still be made out, in spite of the alterations and rebuilding carried out over the centuries. The massive façade in squared blocks of stone, arises from a nucleus of cottages; nearby is the **Church of St. Christine** (XII century). In this building very little of the original character can still be seen, since it has been totally altered by reconstruction works.

1

1. The porticoes façade of the Parish Church of St. Pancras; 2. Panorama of the hills in northern Chianti (with the Pergolato Castle in the foreground). 2

Gabbiano Castle, this suggestive fortified complex is rightly numbered among the most characteristic castles on the Chianti territory. Its origins go back to the XII century but its name was linked for a long time to that of the Soderini family, the Florentine house which proudly opposed the Medicis. Subsequently fallen from power and demeaned, it suffered various changes of ownership until, a few years ago, it was restored to its antique splendour by accurate restoration works. The building as it is seen today is a quadrilateral massive structure with circular towers at the corners and a huge squared tower in a dominating position on the frontal wall, culminating in a sequence of flat-topped battlements.

1. The massive outline of Montefiridolfi Castle rises from among the rustic dwellings; 2. The fertile Chianti land and the vineyards characterize the countryside near Gabbiano; on the opposite page: a view of Gabbiano Castle.

On the previous page: The heavy circular towers which characterize the architecture of Gabbiano Castle; 1. San Casciano Val di Pesa, the Clock-Tower; 2. San Casciano Val di Pesa, a corner of the historic centre; 3. A typical view of the countryside looking towards San Casciano Val di Pesa from Chianti: it is enlivened by the presence of vines, olives and cypresses.

1

2

3

TAVARNELLE VAL DI PESA

The locality, which numbers 6.841 inhabitants, is situated on the border of the actual Classic Chianti area, even though a large part of its Communale territory is included.

The central nucleus of Tavarnelle extends along the two sides of the via Cassia; and this explains the origin of its name: in fact *Tabernulae* is believed to have formed a posting station on this important artery which in Roman times connected the capital city of the Empire with the ancient town of *Florentia*. Towards the end of the VIII century the place was cited in official documents as *Tavernulae*. In the Middle Ages Tavernelle although permanently included in the territories controlled by the Florentines, always remained on the edge of the fierce and bloody disagreements between them and the Sienese. This assertion is supported by the complete absence of fortifications. In a relatively recent era there has been an administrative growth, while in the past these functions were carried out by San Donato in Poggio (which was the chief town until the middle of the XVIII century) and by Badia di Passignano.

The place most frequented by tourists and the most significant from an artistic point of view is the **Church of St. Lucy in the Village (S. Lucia al Borghetto)**. The building is situated on the outskirts of the built-up area and has unmistakable XIII century Franciscan influence. Part of a large convent, it was restructured in the XVI century and restored at the end of the last century. The interior, composed of a single nave retains the gothic design and houses a large number of works of art. There are several frescoes by Sienese painters, a *Crucifix* by a pupil of Giotto, a painting by Neri di Bicci portraying *The Annunciation* and a *Crucifix* in wood in the style of Donatello.

On the previous page: an angle of the massive walls surrounding San Casciano Val di Pesa; 1. San Donato in Poggio, the Parish Church; 2. Tavarnelle Val di Pesa, the Church of St. Lucy at Borghetto.

Recommended Excursions in the Vicinity

Parish Church of St. Peter in Bossolo, this ancient place of worship rose up in all probability in the paleoChristian period although the first known information about it dates from the X century. The building, in Roman form, was concluded with the addition of a portico in the first half of the XVI century. The belltower next to the church was completed around the middle of the last century. The interior, divided into three aisles, retains marble fragments of the paleoChristian period, besides other interesting artistic representations. Worthy of note are a *Virgin Mary with Child and Saints* by Coppo di Marcovaldo, some XVII century paintings and a 14th century marble sanctuary, realised by Florentine artists.

San Donato in Poggio (On the Hill), this ancient village has beautifully preserved the fabric of medieval urban planning and possesses the unmistakable atmosphere of the typical fortified towns of the Chianti region. Originally mentioned in documents pertaining to the Passignano Abbey (X century) San Donato in Poggio became famous in the XII - XIII centuries when it tried to arrive at a solution to the endemic conflicts which tormented the region. Of the ancient **Castle of San Donato on the Hill** there remain only scant traces, visible in some fragments of the fortified walls and in the characteristic tower, the summit of which is surrounded by a line of brackets. It is worth taking a walk into the heart of the medieval village, made extremely suggestive by the narrow paved streets, by the lovely buildings built in large stones, by the arches, the doors and the silent squares. The 14th century **Church of St. Mary of the Snow (S. Maria della Neve)** houses valuable works of art and is flanked by a slender tower on the top of which is a small belltower. Just outside the built-up area is situated the **Parish Church of San Donato**. The building is divided internally into three parts and denotes an elegant linearity on Romanic lines. There is to be found here a valuable baptismal font, enriched by a glazed terracotta ornament carried out in the first half of the XVI century by Giovanni della Robbia. One should note the lovely battlemented belltower which by the huge size of its construction, reveals the defensive use to which it was originally destined.

On the previous page: A view of the Parish Church of St. Peter in Bossolo towered over by its slender bell-tower; a tower is all that remains of the ancient Castle of San Donato in Poggio (opposite); on the following pages: a lovely picture of the Chianti vineyards near San Donato in Poggio.

Sanctuary of Our Lady of Pietra Cupa, this building is to be located at a short distance from San Donato in Poggio and is part of a vast conventual complex. Its realisation came about in the late Renaissance period (end of XVI century) the church, in the form of a latin cross, is distinguished by the portico on the front and is accompanied by an estimable brick belltower. The interior houses a *Virgin Mary with Child* carried out in affresco work by Paolo Schiavo and some paintings believed to be the work of Domenico Crespi, known as *Il Passignano*.

Passignano Abbey, the serene profile of the Abbey arises as if enchanted on the crest of a thickly cultivated green hillside. The numerous towers and the large number of battlemented buildings around which huddle the dwellings render the scene extremely picturesque, whilst the noble and massive presence of the cypress trees confers to the surroundings a bewitched atmosphere. From far off the construction as a whole has the aspect of a well-fortified village which contrasts with the real nature of the premises which have been, over the centuries, places of worship and labour for the monks. It is believed that the site on which the Abbey arose was already occupied in Etruscan times; archeological findings have however ascertained the presence of man in the Roman period. The first official mention dates from the IX century: starting in the XI century life at the Abbey was moulded by St. Giovanni Gualberto the founder of the Vallombrosani monks who died here and was buried in 1703. Throughout the Middle Ages the complex was not spared from forays, pillage and distruction. Reinforced in the XIV and XVII centuries the Abbey has been conserved until our time and constitutes a fundamental stage in understanding institutional monasteries in Tuscany. The **Church of St. Michael** has at its highest point a marble sculpture representing the *archangel Michael* (XIII century). Inside the church can be admired numerous paintings by the 16th - 17th century artist Domenico Crespi, born here and therefore nicknamed *Il Passignano*. Also worthy of note are a statue by G.B. Caccini portraying *S. Giovanni Gualberto*, a reliquary bust of the same person (sacresty) and some paintings by Allori and his pupils. In the **Parish of St. Biagio** are conserved fragments of affresco paintings from the XV century in the style of Ghirlandaio.

On the preceding pages: San Donato in Poggio, a medieval doorway; San Donato in Poggio, a medieval angle (opposite); on page 100: 1. The Sanctuary of Our Lady of Pietra Cupa; 2. The many-towered group of Passignano Abbey; on page 101: San Donato in Poggio, the bell-tower of the Chiesa di S. Maria della Neve.

The Vines, The Grape Harvest, The Wine.

The following pages illustrate some aspects of wineproduction in the Chianti district, showing the vines, various types of grapes, bottled wine and some of the stages

The Aiola lies on a pleasant panoramic road that leads from Vagliagli to Radda.
It is known since the XII the century for its taking part in the heroic resistence of Siena against the troups of Emperor Charles V, allied of Cosimo I, duke of Florence. In the 17th century it has been trasformed in residence and still nov shows traces of the old medieval castle.

(Photo Aiola)

INDEX

Editing:
Editing Studio - Pisa

English Translation:
Rhiannon Lewis

Graphics and Lay out:
Andrea Zottele - Bolzano

Front and Back Cover Photographs:
G. Barone, G. Valdes, R. Filippin, Fattoria della Aiola

editions ITALCARDS bologna - italy

Printed at the printing works
LA FOTOMETALGRAFICA EMILIANA SPA
San Lazzaro di Savena - Bologna
Printed in Italy